DONNA'S STORY

A Journey Through Alzheimer's Disease

John Knapp

FriesenPress

Suite 300 - 990 Fort St
Victoria, BC, V8V 3K2
Canada

www.friesenpress.com

Copyright © 2017 by John Knapp
First Edition — 2017

First Front Cover Photo by Wolfgang Knauer

All rights reserved.

No part of this publication may be reproduced in any form, or by any means, electronic or mechanical, including photocopying, recording, or any information browsing, storage, or retrieval system, without permission in writing from FriesenPress.

ISBN
978-1-4602-9936-4 (Hardcover)
978-1-4602-9937-1 (Paperback)
978-1-4602-9938-8 (eBook)

1. BIOGRAPHY & AUTOBIOGRAPHY

Distributed to the trade by The Ingram Book Company

Donna is on a long journey through Alzheimer's disease. It is like a mountain road with many twists and turns, heading steadily downhill. There are no places to make a U-turn; no rest stops. As Donna's caregiver, I too am on this road, but I am fortunate. I am equipped with a set of brakes that I can apply periodically to enable me to stop and rest. I could even get off the road entirely, should I wish, but that would mean abandoning Donna, for Donna has no set of brakes.

This book describes the past seven years we have spent together on that road, sharing moments of tears and horror as well as some happy episodes. At times we questioned, "Is this all just a mistake—a nightmare from which we will soon awake?" No! The journey continues and it is relentless. Today, Donna is in care and her anxieties have eased, but her family, friends and I still accompany her on that road.

I do not offer suggestions or guidelines as to how you might manage yourself on a similar journey, as either victim or caregiver. All I can offer is some comfort that you are not alone. Alzheimer's affects everyone differently. Your stories will all be unique.

This is Donna's story.

WHAT IS ALZHEIMER'S DISEASE?

As you will have guessed from the title, Donna, my wife, is suffering from Alzheimer's disease. Obviously she cannot write her story for herself, but I feel it should be told, if for no other reason than perhaps it might help ease the pain and trauma of another person, as well as their family and friends. In truth, this is not just Donna's story but *our* story; what we have been through together over the past few years.

Dementia, in all its forms, is a fatal disease. But it is not to be suffered by the poor, unsuspecting victims alone. All of us who surround them must share the fear, anguish, dismay and prolonged helplessness brought on by this dreaded disease.

I would like to begin by briefly describing dementia or, more specifically, late-onset Alzheimer's disease, as I understand it. I am neither doctor nor scientist. I am an untrained layman and caring husband trying to make some sense of the course of events that have passed, and to hopefully prepare myself for the stages that follow—the days, weeks, perhaps months and years to come. My information may be faulty in some areas. If so, I hope you'll forgive me.

There are many different varieties (and sub-varieties) of dementia, with late-onset Alzheimer's being the most prevalent, closely followed by Lewy Body dementia. Other diseases that we don't normally associate with dementia include Parkinson's disease, Down's syndrome and Huntington's disease. There are hundreds more varieties, and the incidence of dementia is increasing rapidly in our society.

Alzheimer's begins in the hippocampus area of the brain, right at the top of the brainstem and spinal column. Cells begin to die without being replaced by new cells as they naturally would in the normal process of all living things. The hippocampus is the area of the brain where the events we experience during the waking day are stored. While sleeping at night, those events are sorted, filtered and filed to other parts of the brain—the long-term memory areas. With the death of cells in the hippocampus, those experiences are not being transferred—at least, not correctly.

As the disease progresses, it moves to the frontal lobe of the brain, the part associated with thinking, imagination, speech, cognitive functions like using a calculator or solving a puzzle and mechanical functions like reading a clock, operating a TV, a phone or a stove.

Slowly, the disease proceeds over the top central cortex region and mood swings begin, some motor functions begin to fade, like using a knife and fork, and sometimes bathroom hygiene becomes a problem. As the disease moves towards the back of the brain, body awareness, hearing, eyesight, touch, taste and smell begin to suffer; hallucinations are not uncommon. It isn't as though those skills disappear. It is more like the brain misinterprets the signals and things don't appear as they are in reality—hence the hallucinations. Physical objects might become lopsided. A toilet might be leaning to one side, or not seen at all because it is the same colour as the surrounding wall. The complex function of standing up and walking will begin to deteriorate.

Finally, Alzheimer's reaches the lower back portion, the cerebellum, where basic motor functions are controlled. Soon the victim will forget how to tell the heart to beat or the lungs to breathe—and life ends. The process is not believed to be painful to the sufferer, which is, perhaps, its only consolation.

There are, of course, thousands of greater details known by science today, but these are generally beyond my ken so I will be wise and not expound on the little I know. Suffice to say there is no known cure, and, even more to the point, there is no way to reverse the process.

Alzheimer's disease begins about twenty years before anyone notices anything out of the ordinary. That's somewhat understandable considering the brain consists of about 500 billion cells. From the first time odd bits of behaviour are noticed (not just the simple memory lapses we all suffer from as we age), it can take from eight to twelve years to elapse. I have known those who succumbed in only three years, and others who have clung to their lives for twenty years. Other forms of dementia follow different schedules of deterioration.

Survival time is hugely dependent on the patient's general health. Factors that can significantly shorten a person's life span are heart disease and diabetes. Those diseases are not directly related to dementia, but will influence the body's ability to fend off the relentless attacks. Obesity adversely affects all ailments, including heart disease and diabetes, as well as Alzheimer's and the other dementias.

Over the years, since first discovering Alzheimer's disease in Donna, there have been long periods of great anguish, first for Donna, then for me, and also for all our friends and relatives, because I have not been silent. As the years passed, I have inundated everyone within email reach with regular chronological updates. I am happy to report that today, in 2016, I am certain that Donna is not in physical pain or mental anguish. However, in varying degrees, that burden remains for the rest of us to bear as we watch her continue to regress.

I wasn't quite sure where to begin. I didn't know if I should start her story from the time her neurologists accepted a diagnosis of Alzheimer's, or from when I believed I first saw the symptoms. I wondered if I should go back twenty years further, seeing that scientists today believe the disease starts at least twenty years before anyone notices symptoms. But I have decided to begin Donna's story at the beginning, or at least from the time she and I first met. I will be brief with my ancient history.

ANCIENT HISTORY
1962 – 1980

Donna and I met in 1962. She was seventeen; I was twenty. She was just beginning her career as a dance teacher for Grace MacDonald in Vancouver. Throughout her childhood, dancing had been her prime interest. She was an excellent dancer, and Grace considered her good enough to become one of her principal teachers. Over the following four years, Donna and I fell in love and were married in 1966.

In 1967, Donna's teaching career unfortunately ended when Grace retired and closed her studio. Within a year, Donna and I decided to pursue one of our early dreams—an extended holiday in Europe. We hopped on Via Rail, travelled across Canada to Newfoundland, then flew to Scotland. This holiday became one of life's exciting adventures, turning into more of an emigration than a holiday. We stayed in Europe for fourteen years.

During those years in Europe, the closest Donna came to continuing her dreams of dancing was to teach yoga for her workmates at Ovaltine. I was more fortunate with my career in those early years. I had joined the fledgling computer services industry and was able to enjoy fruitful employment anywhere in Europe. By the time we returned to Canada in 1980, Donna was ready to come home. Her father had just passed away from dementia.

1981 – 1992

In 1981, Donna and I settled in the Vancouver area once again. Through most of these years Donna pursued a career as a freelance travel agent and did nothing in the dance or entertainment industry. Her warm and friendly personality brought her success in the difficult field of sales and travel.

During those years we had both enjoyed reasonably good health. However, in 1987, Donna found a lump on her breast. The medical community reacted instantly. The biopsy indicated malignancy, and the lump was quickly removed. In those days, cancer was automatically considered a fatal disease with only a few reported recoveries. The days, weeks and months that followed were an endurance run, full of stress for all of us, but mostly for Donna. She must have set her mind to defeat the dreaded "C" because, on the day of her operation, against the advice of her doctors, she quit smoking—a habit she had followed for nearly forty years. After the operation, Donna's health rapidly improved and she was back at work within six weeks. It wasn't long before her doctors proclaimed her "cancer free." There is no scientific evidence to support what I say next, but I will note that Donna's cancer experience occurred approximately twenty years prior to my noticing the onset of Alzheimer's.

1993 – 2007

In 1993, Donna rediscovered dance as a career. While taking some tap dance lessons as a method of exercise, Donna was "discovered." Her new teacher was so enamoured with her skill and style that she asked Donna to teach for her. I remember conversations with Donna at this time. She didn't really believe she still had the teaching skills, but was excited to give it a try. Her students loved her and she began creating some innovative ideas.

Six years later, Donna and I had more conversations. She wondered if she could succeed in building her own dance school. After a summer spent working out the financial aspects and a summer brewing some creative choreography ideas, Footloose Dance was formed. In 1999, the company was started with Donna as its only teacher and a base of thirty tiny new dancers. It worked! The school expanded to 260 students in 2007, and Donna's reputation for creativity in choreography and staging grew throughout the industry.

Timing was perfect for me to help. I had just retired from my career in IT (the latest term for computer services) so I took on roles as accountant, business manager and occasionally even receptionist for Donna. We worked well together.

In 2007, at the age of sixty-three, Donna decided to sell Footloose Dance and retire.

2007 – 2009

The next two years or so were dedicated to enjoying our retirement. We renovated our kitchen and bathroom, as well as our garden, so we might both enjoy some years together in our home. And Donna did not intend to stop dancing. Throughout the past years teaching, and the "Footloose" years, Donna had never performed—only taught. So now she joined a senior's tap dance class at a local community centre and performed again for the first time since she was a teenager.

Christmas 2009 was when I first noticed some peculiar memory lapses in Donna. Not normal things like forgetting someone's name but knowing it is somewhere in the back of your mind and will emerge in time. These lapses were different. We would be discussing what we were going to make for dinner, and ten minutes later Donna didn't remember the conversation at all and swore it never happened.

2010 – NO DIAGNOSIS

For the first few months of 2010, our lives were happy and normal. Memory lapses, as described above, were rare but did occasionally occur. Donna didn't recognize her lapses and if ever I discussed them with her, she became indignant and resentful. So I mostly said nothing; just worried and observed.

At Easter, we visited my brother Dave and his wife in Kelowna where, as was our custom, we played bridge in the evenings. After one of our games, Dave approached me. Both he and Barb had noticed peculiar types of memory lapses during the card game. That was the first time the word Alzheimer's was spoken, but I had been thinking about it since Christmas.

In June, lapses were more frequent, mostly as the day wore on and tiredness grew. So far I had still not discussed it with Donna. I was unsure how to approach the topic, but I received encouragement from Dave. I needed to do it soon. A week or so later, Donna and I had our first discussion, and I learned that she had also been noticing some memory problems and was a little worried about it. She said TV programs watched the previous evening were sometimes not remembered the following day.

Over the next few weeks, Donna and I discussed Alzheimer's openly. She knew it was fatal, but also that it could take as long as twenty years to progress to the end. Donna was sixty-five, in good health, and she joked that she would probably die of old age before Alzheimer's took her.

Finally, in July, Donna discussed these problems with her doctor. I was not there, so I am not sure how the conversation went, but at some point Donna mentioned she had Petit Mal (a mild version of epilepsy) as a child. Her doctor scheduled a CT scan, an EEG and an appointment with a neurologist. Nothing conclusive came from the scans, and it was three months before she could see the neurologist.

In September, Donna and I travelled by car to Saskatchewan to visit her sister. During this three-week period, there appeared to be no memory lapses and everything seemed normal.

However, when at home, I could see her anxiety was rising. She would often wake up angry, and I occasionally saw her crying to herself when she thought no-one noticed; natural reactions, I felt, to living under the threat of Alzheimer's. At this point there was no formal diagnosis, just the worries of the two of us who knew nothing about the disease except its final outcome.

In November, Donna saw her neurologist, who put her through various tests for Alzheimer's. He asked her to draw a clock and put the arms on pointing to a specified time. Another test was to mention five things and ask Donna to remember them for later in the discussion. When asked again ten minutes later, she couldn't remember the five items. However, the doctor declared, "No Alzheimer's disease," "Just a case of mild dementia." I had no idea what that meant, but at least there was an immediate improvement in Donna's anxiety, and a reduction in the periods of anger in the days and weeks that followed.

2011 – DIAGNOSIS EPILEPSY

In the first couple of months following her visit to the neurologist, Donna's stress levels decreased, but the memory lapses increased in frequency. We both noticed that on occasions when we were at the theatre, visiting friends for the evening, or having friends visit us, the memory lapses didn't occur. They only seemed to happen when we were home alone, and only in the evening from dinner time onward. During the day, all functions seemed normal. Donna continued to drive her car, run errands, visit friends, play bridge and take her tap dance classes. At home, I was the principal cook, but we worked as a partnership in the kitchen.

However, Donna's doctor wasn't any more pleased than we were about her neurologist's diagnosis—"just a case of mild dementia"—so an appointment was set to obtain a second opinion. In May, we visited a second neurologist, this time with me in attendance. (In fact, I have attended all Donna's doctor's appointments from that time on.) In conversation with the neurologist, Donna again described her childhood Petit Mal, so the doctor scheduled another EEG. I explained the nature of the lapses as I saw them; how they occurred in the evening while watching TV, and how she would sometimes take on a glazed look, not really being aware of her surroundings. A bit like the childhood "absence seizure" typical of Petit Mal. The neurologist renamed the lapses as "spells," and asked if I might video some occasions when Donna was in this state.

Over the next few months, Donna had her EEG and I did manage a couple of videos, although I really had no idea whether that moment would result in a memory spell until we reviewed it the next day. I'm not really sure how effective that action was.

In June, we again motored to Saskatchewan and Donna did a little of the driving. However, she was now very uncomfortable behind the wheel and she has not driven since that time. We didn't discuss details, but I noticed she was having trouble making decisions regarding all the functions necessary to drive: footwork, what to do with her hands and awareness of all her surroundings, especially traffic. Donna's capability behind the wheel was noticeably poorer than six months earlier.

During the summer of 2011, Donna's memory spells began to increase again, happening sometimes earlier in the afternoon when she was helping prepare dinner. Her sleeping was also becoming erratic. She occasionally got extremely tired and slipped off to bed about 6:00 or 7:00 PM without dinner. Then, waking three or four hours later, she might try to reach the bathroom and get lost on the way. Completely disoriented, she would head for the wrong room, or the closet, or even try to open the front door and work her way outside. Later in the same night, if she awoke again to use the bathroom, all functions would be normal. On other occasions she might sleep a continuous twelve or fourteen hours.

My general observation during those days was that Donna's stress and anxiety were again rising. She was fully aware of what was happening to her body, had no idea what to do about it and was simply frightened. The doctors weren't solving anything.

In August, we met once more with Donna's neurologist. The EEG tests were negative. But he thought that because Donna's spells only occurred in the evening, while both the EEG tests had been given in the morning, there may have been some correlation. He stated that Donna's childhood Petit Mal had returned and so prescribed a regimen of drugs to attempt to control her epilepsy. He believed that with the proper medication the epilepsy seizures ("spells" were now renamed "seizures") could be adequately managed. Donna's relief was immediate. Epilepsy was not a fatal disease; it could be managed, if not cured.

I wanted to feel happy, but was not quite convinced of his diagnosis. To me, Donna's experiences were definitely not seizures—at least, nothing like I pictured an epileptic seizure to be.

In September, Donna began with an entry-level dosage of Keppra. By the end of the month, there was no decrease in the number of seizures, but there was a marked increase in Donna's level of tiredness. She could no longer enjoy any after-dinner games or conversation.

She was typically very angry with me when she got up in the morning, but eating breakfast usually calmed things down. Her periods of depression increased, as did her tearful moments. Donna knew her brain was in trouble.

In October, after mentioning I saw no visible sign of improvement, Donna was switched to a second epilepsy drug, Carbamazepine. Bad things immediately began to happen, including uncontrollable muscle spasms in her arms and legs that frightened us both.

She was quickly returned to Keppra, and, in compliance with the plan to increase her dosage, the quantity was doubled. This continued until the end of the year, but what was originally considered undue tiredness could now be called "extreme tiredness." Donna was becoming disoriented almost every night when waking and trying to find the bathroom. We both felt that the sooner she could come off the Keppra, the better.

2012 – DIAGNOSIS ALZHEIMER'S

Donna was now tired all the time. Her left eye was developing a tic. She had sharp, migraine-like pains in various spots in her head, brief, shooting pains in her legs and feet and was almost always constipated. It was nearly impossible to separate issues that related to the epilepsy, those that were a result of the medication side effects, and those that were psychosomatic, caused by her extreme stress and anxiety.

Other drugs were now being introduced to offset the side effects of the medications. Senna, to help with the constipation, vitamin B12 injections to reduce the seizures, and extremely high doses of vitamin D to relieve the tiredness. We both believed with all our hearts that this was not good, and not the way to go. Those days were very difficult. As well as the high anxiety, Donna's self-esteem was dropping rapidly. She felt she was not worth all the effort and attention.

In late January, Donna had her next visit with her neurologist. He was not happy with the effects of the Keppra and decided to change it once again, this time to Lamictal. But he offered a warning that Lamictal could induce a body rash that, if not relieved, might prove fatal. It was introduced by first lowering the dose of Keppra to wean Donna off slowly, followed by a small initial dose of Lamictal, to be increased as the body got used to the drug.

He also suggested that the vitamins B12 and D should be stopped, then concluded with the comment that he was not fully confident with his epilepsy diagnosis, that Donna's problem might not be neurological and that hypo-glycaemia and other diabetes-related issues should be considered.

As soon as Donna received the lower dose of Keppra, all her symptoms disappeared. No more constipation! No more tiredness! And her anxieties immediately reduced.

Then the Lamictal was started. For the first ten days—no problem. When the dosage increased, all hell broke loose. Donna awoke one morning with a tactile rash all over her body. Little bumps that certainly spelled problems for her. No doctors available as this was Sunday, so it was off to Emergency. The ER doctors would not override the neurologist's wishes but advised that the rash likely was a side effect—a possibly lethal side effect—of the drug. However, Donna and I *could* override the neurologist's decisions, so we immediately stopped the Lamictal.

You can guess where Donna's anxieties were then—and mine.

In February, we had another meeting with her neurologist. He agreed with the cessation of Lamictal, and decided to stop the Keppra as well. At this meeting he also said that perhaps Alzheimer's (a word not mentioned in almost eighteen months) should not be ruled out, and that route ought to be investigated. He scheduled Donna for an MRI.

With the cessation of the epilepsy drugs, Donna's mood immediately changed for the better: there was no more tiredness, her anxiety dropped, her anger was reduced and she generally felt a lot better. She started Aricept, a medication for Alzheimer's, with no initial reaction. Of course, she was still suffering the memory lapses ("seizures" now returned to "lapses") that now occurred every day. Donna still enjoyed TV, but virtually all programs that required remembering what had transpired, meant nothing to her. She couldn't even enjoy her favourite program, "So You Think You Can Dance," because she couldn't remember anything about the contestants. She only really enjoyed programs like "Ellen DeGeneres" because it consisted of short humorous skits with known actors.

With Donna's neurologist now thinking that Alzheimer's was a possibility, we discussed the value of coconut oil. Don't laugh! Coconut oil had been reported to help induce the liver to produce ketones. Ketones are supposedly an alternative food for brain cells, after glucose, and it was thought that Alzheimer's might really be a kind of Type Three Diabetes, where the brain cells die because insulin is ineffective in delivering the appropriate amounts of glucose to the necessary cells. Ketones seemed to fit the bill. The doctor pointed out that this was an unproven theory, but that it wouldn't do harm once we realized that coconut oil was a saturated fat and could contribute to cholesterol build up.

Donna was next moved to a double dose of Aricept. Again, the impact was immediate—almost continuous diarrhea. A dose taken at bedtime meant she was up all night with diarrhea. It also created leg cramps that occurred at regular intervals during the night. This time, Donna made her own decision to stop the drug. Effect? Everything returned to normal.

With the next visit to her neurologist in March, he confirmed that Donna's decision to stop the drug was correct. He also said the MRI test was not conclusive, and was just showing a minor bit of brain atrophy. He noticed that Donna's general well-being had improved and suggested that no medication was the route to follow for the time being.

From May to August, things progressed normally. We asked her neurologist if perhaps alcohol (red wine) might have an adverse effect. He was non-committal, and no other doctor had even suggested such a thing. We still noticed that knowledge of events in the evening, theatre, visits, etc., seemed to be retained the next day; memory lapses were really only occurring at home. Generally, lapses still happened, but there was no noticeable degradation of motor capabilities. These topics were regular discussions between Donna and me—they were not just my observations. For both of us, it was a relief to be off all the medications.

In September, we visited her neurologist again. He noticed that Donna was still reading and doing crossword puzzles, noted that she had started tap dance classes again, and was beginning to learn the piano. All good things, so he prescribed no medications. Next visit would be in March.

At this time, I was able to leave Donna alone for three or four hours at a time without fear of her getting anxious or dismayed and wandering through the neighbourhood.

Through October and November, I noticed some deterioration in Donna's general awareness. Yet somehow she still managed to get herself in tip-top shape, mentally, before visits to her neurologist. She really wasn't reading. She couldn't get past page one, because by the time she got to page two, she had forgotten what transpired on page one. One crossword puzzle could take her a month. Her tap dance classes petered out in September and she would not be restarting them in January as she hoped and planned. Donna continued her bridge club with our neighbour; her bridge-playing skills had certainly deteriorated, but these were all friends. Her piano training was limited to the one song she had learned six months earlier. There would be no second song, although we both tried to make it happen. I began to feel we needed an earlier visit to her neurologist than the scheduled March appointment.

In December, Donna had a medical emergency while I was not home. I had been at her best friend's funeral—Donna felt she was too emotional to handle it, so she decided to stay home. She called me on my cellphone, and I could tell she was deeply troubled and unable to calm down. I was stuck in rush-hour traffic at least thirty minutes away. I told her I would meet her at Emergency and called an ambulance. When I tried to call Donna back, her phone was busy.

When I arrived at the hospital, she had not yet been picked up, so I hurried home. My neighbour told me the ambulance had just left. The house was a shambles! TV blaring! All lights on! Bathroom a mess! Doors wide open! The phone had not been hung up, so that was why I couldn't comfort her during my race to the hospital. I went back to the hospital and she was there.

She was strapped to the stretcher suffering from extreme anxiety. She was running a high fever, shivering uncontrollably and very cold. The nurses were trying to cool her down because of the fever, all the time attaching wires, tubes and other paraphernalia to test her vital functions— actions not conducive to easing anxiety, hers or mine. Slowly, slowly, she calmed down. She spent the night, and managed to get a little sleep with me sitting beside her. We left the next morning with no adequate explanation of what occurred.

In a December meeting with her neurologist, there were no new topics discussed. The doctor took Donna through the comprehensive tests for Alzheimer's, including those tests I described earlier. This time I was in attendance and was completely shocked by Donna's inability to draw a clock or tell the time from an old-fashioned dial clock. She was okay with a digital clock. These tests took a long time, and I was shaken by the results. I was not expecting the level of disorientation, or her difficulty with mechanical or related things. Donna could no longer use her computer—I thought she just didn't want to. She couldn't turn the TV on or off or change the channels. There were dozens of other things that I had just begun to realize were a problem for her. She couldn't operate the stove or dishwasher and couldn't make coffee. I was very surprised that she was able to call me on my cell that day of the visit to Emergency. Then I remembered. She had managed the first call, but didn't think to hang up so she might receive a subsequent call from me.

The diagnosis from her neurologist was finally set on Alzheimer's disease and a new term entered our vocabulary—"caregiver." I was now Donna's full time caregiver and obviously couldn't leave her for more than a couple of hours, a fact I hadn't quite realized until that moment.

Alzheimer's!

In my mind, I had believed that to be Donna's problem, right from the beginning—way back at Christmas 2009. But I was not an expert, just a layman who knew nothing at all about the disease. It was absolutely imperative to follow the advice of the doctors who were reticent to commit to a diagnosis without the science to back them up. I understood their point of view. But it took us down paths that were unfortunate. Neither Donna nor I felt any animosity towards the medical profession—we understood they were doing their best in a largely unknown field of science.

But it was time for me to study and learn something about this dreaded disease. In my brain, I had some sense of what was to follow, but my heart had not yet accepted that future. Donna also seemed to understand and accept that she had Alzheimer's ("accept" is probably not the right word).

2013 – THE WAITING GAME

We were now entering 2013, the fourth year since I first noticed anomalies in Donna's behaviour that I felt were the onset of Alzheimer's. Up to this time, there was no noticeable degradation in Donna's physical capabilities and motor skills. She could still dance extremely well, even if she couldn't remember the choreography. The steps had been in her brain since childhood; only the choreography was new and unable to be retained.

And Donna and I were both giving thanks that the era of those horrendous drugs was behind us. The doctors were trying to do their best, but now that the diagnosis was Alzheimer's, we both felt it was best to leave the drugs behind. It had just become a waiting game. We knew the best that could be achieved was to slow down the progress of the disease, but those drugs had a devastating effect on Donna's physical well-being. This realization was having a high emotional cost to us both, but hopefully there would be no physical pain for Donna.

For the first half of that year, our lives progressed more or less normally. One of the changes I noticed in 2013 was that Donna seemed to have lost her understanding of time. For her, there was no past, present and future—everything was the present. This was demonstrated when she tried to read our appointments calendar. She didn't understand that events written there will occur, or did occur, on days to come or days gone by. To Donna, everything was today!

Our home life was not very happy. We were becoming more like hermits. We did visit friends occasionally, but we went out only rarely, mainly just to do the necessary grocery shopping, etc. We no longer visited the theatre or saw movies. Restaurants offered less enjoyment for Donna than before; she sometimes misbehaved, and we once had to leave early. We didn't go for walks anymore. Donna didn't seem to have the stamina for even the one-kilometer walk around Como Lake that we used to enjoy regularly. I could go out shopping on my own (get a haircut, visit the bank) because I didn't really worry about leaving Donna alone for an hour or two. Her anxiety didn't build and she didn't seem to have any desire to wander. But her self-esteem was again very low.

Now, as well as her issues with anger before breakfast in the morning, she was also experiencing more dramatic mood swings. These occurred typically around 4:00 or 5:00 PM—the "sundown" syndrome the experts talked about. A mood swing would happen while we were happily discussing something. Suddenly, almost in the middle of a sentence, Donna would explode. It might be just a word taken out of context. She would insult me and pick a fight, seemingly just to raise my ire and solicit some response. I sometimes took the bait, then regretted it after a half-hour of argument.

One of the things we had to do that year was find a new GP for Donna. After meeting with her GP a couple of times the year before, I realized she didn't really have any empathy for Donna and didn't seem to know how to help her. When Donna asked her to offer an explanation of what occurred that night at the Emergency, she actually scolded Donna, telling her she had no right to question the ministrations of the medical community. Perhaps she didn't really understand Alzheimer's disease. Changing doctors was an extremely difficult thing to do because there were so few who took on new patients. It took us until June to be successful.

In September, we decided to repeat our "honeymoon" train journey across Canada, in the hopes of recalling past joys of our youth. It was not to be. The jerky, noisy movements of the train were traumatic to Donna, and she didn't really sleep through any night. We did the trip in four legs, each leg being two days and nights. Donna felt great relief whenever we disembarked, and it became very difficult to convince her to get back on again for the next leg. The train was very long. Twice Donna got lost and I found her, sobbing, seven or eight cars up the line. Once, I feared she got off and was about to be left behind when the train pulled out.

In retrospect, there were some terrific moments as well on that rail trip. Through all the years I've known Donna, she has been a happy, demure, quiet and somewhat subdued person. One afternoon on our train journey, there was a young singer/guitarist who joined our coach for an hour's entertainment. Donna was in seventh heaven. She got up and danced in front of everyone in the car, loudly singing "Hallelujah," her current favourite song. What a wonderful and unexpected outburst! What happiness she experienced!

In December, we met with her neurologist, who commented once again that he saw no deterioration in Donna's well-being, but at least he prescribed no medication. Next visit— April.

2014 – A CONFUSING YEAR

In April of 2014, we had our last meeting with Donna's neurologist. He had scheduled another EEG, and the results again proved negative. He commented once more that he could see no deterioration in Donna's well-being—in fact, he saw no change over the previous two years. He stated that he was no longer convinced that Donna had Alzheimer's, could do nothing for her, and decided to pass Donna over to the senior's Geriatric Services Clinic, who might be able to help. This just served to confuse us both. If not Alzheimer's, then what? The perhaps fortunate, perhaps unfortunate, result of his comment was that Donna no longer believed she had Alzheimer's disease. That relieved some of her stress, so I was all for it. But one of the unfortunate effects was taking away his support—support that Donna fully trusted and respected. Even her favourite doctor had "rejected" her.

The doctors at the geriatric clinic proved to be very good and supportive to both Donna and me. Donna was assigned a dementia expert and a psychologist—the psychologist was probably there to help me as Donna's caregiver. Donna was immediately given a full physical exam, including all the requisite bloodwork, X-rays and even a genetic test to ensure some of her complaints were not physical medical issues but psychosomatic, as a result of her years of trauma. The assessment concluded that Donna did, indeed, have late-onset Alzheimer's disease and that she was in approximately the middle of the second of three stages of the disease. It helped in my understanding of the disease, but it didn't matter to Donna. She knew she no longer had Alzheimer's—her neurologist said so. Overall, Donna's anxieties lessened because the doctors at the geriatric clinic were so understanding and helpful. She could talk to them and they listened. Donna began to smile again.

People at the clinic also told us about another aspect of our situation. They said we must get our financial and legal position settled immediately. It was necessary to set up an enduring power of attorney over Donna, as well as a type of medical power of attorney called a Rep 9 agreement. The Rep 9 agreement allowed Donna to state, in legal terms, how she wanted to be treated by the medical community as she progressed down the path of Alzheimer's. It was the modern equivalent of the living will. All this was necessary while Donna could still understand the implications.

Donna and I also needed to ensure our wills were how we wished them to be. With the help of Donna's brother and my brother, along with lawyers, we managed to set up the power of attorney and Rep 9. The lawyer's comment was that we were just in time for him to accept Donna's signature on those legal documents, but he would not be prepared to alter her will, believing Donna to not be cognizant enough to understand those implications, even in the spring of 2014.

Another recommendation from the geriatric clinic was that we should sell our home and move to a senior's facility on the ground floor and within easy walking distance to amenities. My feeling about this was that neither Donna nor I were ready for a senior's facility, and such a disruption to our environment would completely disorient her and adversely affect her well-being.

Donna's doctor at the clinic prescribed another version of Aricept medication to help delay the onslaught of Alzheimer's. Instead of a pill that Donna already knew would upset her stomach, the prescription was for a patch to be applied to her skin, where the drug could be absorbed without impacting the digestive system. It needed to be applied with an "opsite" bandage. We brought the materials home, but I was very reluctant to try them. Even the opsite bandage had its perils. It needed to be applied to different parts of her body without repeating any part for thirty days. I was dismayed. What should I do? I knew my feelings were selfish; I didn't want to prolong Donna's existence at these costs. Was that fair to Donna?

I spoke to my doctor and he eased my mind a little. First, he reminded me that I had already lost Donna. There was no recovery from the damages already done to her brain and those that were going to be done. He also pointed out that the medications were designed to help those in the early stages of Alzheimer's, and would likely not be that efficacious in Donna's case. And Donna still had horrible memories of the previous drugs. I never did apply that medication.

Through the latter half of 2014, we were both still just waiting.

Donna had always been a happy and social sort of person, liking people to visit her, visiting others, and any sort of party, conversing easily with all people. Donna still strongly desired to join in social events, but they always deteriorated in her mind, and we generally left early to allow her to relax and relieve her tensions and anxieties. On our way to a visit, Donna wouldn't visualize any difficulties, just the great memories she had of past times together. At the end of the visit, she was extremely saddened and often angry.

For thanksgiving that year, we visited with Donna's brother, Bruce, and his family. For me, it was a typical day in our lives at that time, but it completely shocked Bruce. He had never seen Donna at her roughest moments until that Saturday. We arrived about 3:00 PM, and present were Bruce, Shirley, their daughter Amanda with her new boyfriend and his mother—altogether, there were seven of us. Conversations were tense at the beginning until we all got to know each other.

As time went on, I saw that Donna was not able to keep up with the chatter and was getting a little agitated. When she came into the conversation, she was only able to talk about the topic remaining in her mind—her dance. And her stories were all mixed up, with events and people out of context. When conversations about dance failed her, she got up and sang songs to us all—trying to find some way to become part of the social group. Donna felt left out, frightened and extremely lonely. She was feeling that her friends no longer liked her, and maybe never did.

When individuals tried to help her with things like directions to the bathroom, friendly help that we all believed should make her feel thankful, she interpreted it as criticism, showing, yet again, that she was making mistakes and getting things wrong.

As that day wore on, Donna became more and more agitated and angry. Eventually, before dinner was over, she became a little violent—aimed primarily at me—and we had to leave. By the time we arrived back home her anger had eased and I helped her to bed at about 6:00 PM. The next day, she remembered nothing of the afternoon before. These experiences, while new to Bruce and Shirley, were fairly regular occurrences at home.

I began to see that Donna's brain did not work at a speed that would allow her to formulate her thoughts and ideas in time to respond to social conversation. She heard all that people said, but it became an unorganized jumble in her mind. It was a bit like a person at a party with a hearing aid. All sounds entered her brain at the same intensity, but she was unable to sift and sort the things people said in time to offer her comments—it was just a cacophony of sounds. This made her frustrated and angry. The only way she could participate was on her terms, on subjects that she still had control over—her singing and dance. You and I have the ability to filter out surrounding sounds, focus on specific people and words and ignore the rest. Donna could no longer do this.

In September, I was diagnosed with a medical problem. My prostate was swollen and would need minor surgery to scrape the sides and enlarge the urethra. This was not urgent, so it was scheduled for some time in 2015. Just another thorn in the side of my anxieties.

In October, we visited the geriatric clinic again to see Donna's psychologist. As mentioned earlier, I understood this person was intended to help me as much as Donna. I needed help! The road ahead was dark and getting darker every day. I had no concrete understanding of what was in store for Donna over the coming months. Was I providing the right kind of care for her? Should I begin to discuss a care facility? With whom? Was there a government authority that covered these things? What financial assistance was available? How did I take care of myself at the same time? And a thousand more questions!

My intention was to continue as Donna's caregiver for as long as possible, but when did I need to call in other resources? The doctors at the clinic were able to help on two main fronts. Yes! The federal government offered financial help in the form of a Disability Tax Credit; and Yes! I should get in touch with Fraser Health immediately. They would provide an "in home" assessment of Donna to see if she was eligible for a long-term care facility. From that assessment, they would register her and place her on the waiting list for accommodation.

But unfortunately…no! They could not prophesy the course of regression Donna was on, to offer insight into what might lie ahead. On my mind at the time was a question that I desperately wanted, and yet didn't want, to ask. What was Donna's life expectancy? All the doctors would do was offer me the statistics: "Alzheimer's disease has an average life expectancy of eight to twelve years." I already knew those statistics, and through the experiences of those near me, I knew that, in reality, the survival range was much wider. They couldn't offer any real help and, in retrospect, perhaps I should not have asked the question.

These were anxiety-ridden times for us both. I tried to maintain an aura of happiness, but was often unsuccessful. I regularly found Donna softly sobbing to herself. Although in denial of Alzheimer's, in her heart she knew what was to come. I now began to understand her anger and her dismay. Her mood swings were completely unpredictable. And yes, I got angry too. My anger simply increased hers, with only negative results. I had to consciously calm myself, speak softly and ignore the outburst that stemmed from that one misplaced word. Then, in about a half-hour, life got back to normal.

The biggest problem we had was that Donna and I hadn't much in common anymore. I didn't take a lot of interest in her clothes, etc. and she didn't take an interest in the things I enjoyed. She couldn't really read books and, lately, could no longer do her crossword puzzles. She couldn't play her favourite games on her computer. We didn't effectively communicate, and she was desperately lonely. She wanted me beside her all the time, and I just couldn't do that as much as she needed.

My next task was to open discussions with Fraser Health, the authority in our area that's responsible for all the public health facilities. They sent an assessment officer to our home to talk to us both. In November 2014, they suggested that Donna should be registered, but that no other action need be taken. I should stay in touch, keep them updated and see how the next months evolved. It was difficult to invite Fraser Health in without telling Donna the background reason. I phrased it in the form of offering respite care for us both, allowing me to go out to doctor, barber, or bank, etc. without needing Donna to accompany me. She could stay home with a friend, relative, or home help person to keep her company.

I planned things we could do together in the early afternoons. Grocery shopping was really a way to offer us both some variety to our days while doing things together. We'd go to Inlet Seafoods in Port Moody for our fish, then it was off to Kin's or T&T for fresh produce, down to Cioffi's on Hastings Street for our meat and deli, over to Oak Barrel to bottle a batch of wine, then finish off at Save-On for the balance. She came home happy from those excursions but extremely tired, and occasionally was in bed before she had a chance to eat dinner.

And Donna's personal hygiene was suffering. She appeared to be frightened of the shower, refused to step in and wouldn't let me help. She also did not wash her hair. I was able to do it for her a couple of times, but that soon stopped. Other bathroom functions were fine. She always washed her face and hands carefully.

At the end of 2014, Donna had her first experience of wandering and getting lost. It was a warm day, and we had enjoyed a great afternoon with lots of smiles and laughter, when Donna decided to go for a walk on the various paths around our garden. This was a normal custom for her. She did it almost daily when the weather was fine, while I stayed in the kitchen preparing something for dinner. Fifteen minutes later, Donna was not back. Unusual. I checked around the garden. No Donna! I called our neighbour because she often liked to visit Elaine. Not there! I was just getting the car out to search for her when I noticed her slowly walking up the hill past our neighbour's driveway. She was sobbing profusely and did not know where she was—even though she was passing the home of our neighbour that she had passed regularly for the past twenty years. She did not recognize our home, only thirty yards away. This was the start of a new era.

"But the days ahead are going to get tougher." I don't know how many times I said that or how many times I wrote it in my multitude of emails I sent over the past years. 2014 was a difficult year.

We were both very depressed; almost despondent. I knew, as did Donna in her heart, that this was a long and scary road with no satisfactory conclusion. We had both set our sights on the medical community to offer a way out, knowing, of course, that there was no way out. The doctor's and related institution's intentions were honorable, but they really didn't seem to understand the emotions we were feeling. Donna clung to me, desperately at times, and the attachment was growing every day as her fears increased. The professional community tried its best this year, but it was difficult for them to accept they had not been able to solve any problems. They could not cure her.

Over the year, as she passed from one specialist to the next, Donna placed a lot of hope on their revelations; those hopes always short lived. By the end of 2014, I felt it was time to say goodbye to the medical teams and work things out for ourselves. As the disease progressed, new ideas and actions would be needed, and I realized I would not be able to provide the care she would need in those later stages. But those decisions, for the moment, were still in the future.

Up to this point in my narrative I have described, principally, how Donna was faring, along with a little of how it was affecting me. But Alzheimer's had not just wielded its hammer on the two of us. Our family and friends also suffered through the years, each with that spot of anguish in their heart for an inability to alleviate Donna's suffering, and often chastised by Donna for their efforts. She usually misinterpreted friendly actions as "You're telling me what to do!" or saying she was doing things wrong. Marylynn—you are Donna's best friend and you tried so many times. Others too! I have a particular respect for you, Bruce. Over the past years, you watched helplessly as your father slowly disintegrated with a different form of dementia. Your mother, too, finally succumbed to Parkinson's—another type of dementia. And now it's the turn of your sister, Donna. There is nothing any of us can do, yet in the end, family provides the strength that will allow us all to come through…except Donna.

Over the years, my family and friends have also offered huge support, as well as much-valued advice. It is often difficult to see the forest for the trees, and I was certainly complacent at times when I should have insisted; procrastinated when I should have acted. As the narrative that follows will show, gentle prods from those close to me eventually stirred me to act despite my terrible fear of taking the steps I knew must follow.

2015 – THE YEAR FROM HELL
JANUARY

At this stage in Donna's Story, I want to move into the present tense. In my mind, the story up to this point in time has felt like history. In 2015, it feels like current events, and becomes more anecdotal, reflecting my current emotions. Perhaps, also at this stage, the story becomes more about me than Donna. How am I coping? This is a traumatic year, culminating in an event that will stay with me for the rest of my life.

At the beginning of the year, I move from sharing a bedroom with Donna to downstairs. It is an important move because I can get some much-needed sleep when she suffers her often turbulent nights.

Today, Donna is still fully aware of everything in her life, although things are often confused and don't make her very happy. She still remembers all of her friends and relatives—even if it sometimes takes a little coaching from me to help stimulate the images in her brain. Those images are beginning to turn grey, and I feel it won't be too long before they disappear forever. But for now, things are still fairly normal.

There are two "Johns" in her life, and I'm not sure what that means. Possibly John ONE is her favourite; he is the one who is always nice to her, while John TWO is an ogre who scolds her about her drinking habits, her unwillingness to take her medications, her refusal to go to bed when she gets up at 3:00 AM, dresses, complete with purse and earrings, and wanders downstairs to wake me. She is wide awake, full of life, and wonders where we are going that day. And she asks, "Do you like how I've combed my hair?"

But I am beginning to notice another change—the next phase, perhaps. Just today I see that Donna is getting more disoriented, beginning to lose her understanding of where things are in her very familiar home. She isn't sure where the TV room is, nor the bathroom…even the bedroom. And the various rooms belong either to Donna or to John. It's John's office, Donna's bedroom, Donna's bathroom, etc. As she moves around our home, articles she comes across have to be put somewhere else, and require an identification to catalogue them as either hers or mine.

Just a night or so ago, Donna comes down to my bedroom about midnight in an extremely agitated state. She can't find me. It takes her a long time to locate me, and she is very frightened, thinking she's alone in the house. I accompany her to her bedroom and stay with her all night. We are eventually able to talk a little. For the first time in all these five years she says to me, "Johnnie, I'm going to die!" I think this realization has just reached her conscious mind and it scares her unimaginably. I'm sure that, in her subconscious, she knows the path Alzheimer's is taking her on, but that night is when the awareness first emerges at a conscious level.

Last night, I decide to room with Donna again. Her fears and anxieties won't abate. I am able to coax her to come to bed and try to sleep for an hour, aided by a couple of Gravols. Nothing works for long. She's up, pacing back and forth between the three or four rooms, reorganizing her shoes for the twentieth time, all the while chattering to me. This is her second sleepless night and looks to be mine as well, but I'm afraid I can't cope with that. I leave to return to my bedroom and hear her pacing for at least a couple of hours. I am beginning to understand that Donna is afraid to go to sleep or, more likely, she lies awake and the horrors in her mind won't let her sleep.

This morning I see she has been very busy reorganizing everything that wasn't fastened down. But she is finally asleep. The elixir of life—sleep!

Where do we go from here? I don't know!

FEBRUARY–APRIL

It is now early February, and my urologist has told me that my prostate operation is scheduled for early March. As soon as all the details are worked out, my anxieties rise once more. What will I do with Donna? She obviously can't remain at home while I am under the knife.

After meeting with Fraser Health, I find they have managed to provide a two-week respite home for Donna at Delta View Care Centre. A care centre! How am I going to get Donna to understand? We have lots of conversations about it, and we also make a visit to the centre, where Donna has a chance to look over the accommodation and talk with some of the staff. It is a spectacular place and Donna seems to understand what is required. She is calm. I think this is going to work.

When the time for my operation comes, we pack a few things for Donna to take with her, and we also pack her new "bible", a song book that includes emails from a long-past student that she has spent the last two months reciting repeatedly to all visitors who have had the patience to listen. She settles in to Delta View with little disruption. My anxieties immediately decrease.

A few days later I have my operation, which seems to be non-invasive and my recovery appears to be progressing on schedule. With the doctor's okay, I drive to Kelowna to visit my brother, Dave, and family. I'm thinking perhaps Donna and I might emigrate to Kelowna, set up home, and be ready to see Donna into a care facility in that beautiful city.

Unfortunately, I suffer a relapse, require three trips to Emergency to correct my prostate problem and need the following three months to recover from the operation. I am not in good health. However, on the third of April, I bring Donna back from her respite care centre and we continue our life. She is happy to be home and, surprisingly, is understanding about my need for rest and recuperation. Things do get back to our state of normalcy, more or less.

But at this time I am not seeing things very straight and believe that my role as Donna's only caregiver is working okay; needs no immediate action. I recognize that the time is near when Donna must move to a permanent care home where she can be assisted twenty-four hours a day, but, here in April, I also assess that the day has not yet arrived, and can wait a while. I believe that my health is back to normal; I can continue without the need for any extra help. I am wrong.

A year earlier, with the help of family, I was able to put Donna's affairs in order through the power of attorney and the Rep 9 agreement. But, after my horrors in Emergency, I am now asking myself the question, "What will happen to Donna if I die prematurely?" I'm seventy-four. It could happen.

Clearly, Donna's affairs are not in order. There will be enough money to take care of her through the sale of our home, but how will that be managed with Donna living in it? She can't live there alone! Who will take care of her? I must make more plans for Donna's care.

So how is Donna faring in this period of my recuperation, my inaction, my procrastination?

After her return home with me a week or so ago, I realize that, although Donna has lots of traumatic times that leave her angry and frightened, most of her world is calm, and she is aware of most of the people and places around her. She still remembers almost everyone, but is certainly frightened of me leaving or discarding her.

Donna's day usually begins about 8:00 AM, shortly after I get up. Every day after breakfast she asks, "Okay! What are we going to do today?" and her frustrations begin to build. Within an hour or two, she is angry and I help her take her medications, one of which is extended-release Seroquel, a drug aimed at calming anxieties. It works very well. By about noon, Donna is completely back to normal and the rest of the day we carry on as usual. We still enjoy lots of laughs together even though she is regularly frustrated because she cannot do many of the things she really wants to do, like preparing dinner with me, or helping our gardener with his spring cleanup. She sings a lot—songs from long ago that I have never heard her sing before. And she appears to know the words, mostly. If I hear her recite, yet again, those long-past emails from one of her dance students, I think I will scream.

At bedtime, Donna is normally very tired and ready to go to her room. I guide her, make sure she is in bed, turn off the light and usually proceed to bed myself. Occasionally, maybe once a week, Donna's anxieties return and she becomes very frightened about getting into bed. She is beginning to have hallucinations that seem to fill her bedroom with other people and she doesn't want to undress in front of them all. Plus, she has a general fear of going to sleep. On these nights, I typically have to leave her, go to bed myself, and await the many visits from her where she demands I get in touch with her mom and dad or brother to come and take her home. This anxiety can continue for many hours and she might not actually get to bed until 4:00 or 5:00 AM.

Donna can no longer function in social situations. I previously described what I think happens to her when trying to join a social conversation. She is able to manage with one or two people at most; she is always extremely pleased to have a visitor, and will happily talk to anyone who will talk to her.

MAY – JUNE

This week, Donna and I again meet the doctors at the geriatric clinic. Donna enjoys talking to them, but it is necessary for me to be in attendance to ensure the information asked by the doctors is correctly answered. Donna will often misunderstand questions or will deliberately mislead, claiming everything is good. I also meet with her GP and her Fraser Health case manager. The topic is always the same, "How is Donna managing?" I am also searching for confirmation that I am doing things that are appropriate for Donna's care.

I ask the question about appropriate care because today, life with Donna is very difficult. Only a month ago, I described how we enjoyed lots of happy times, as well as periods of Donna's mood swings, fears, anxieties, tears, etc. For the most part today, there are very few periods of happiness. Donna usually gets up angry, and it typically takes a couple of hours or more before any conversations occur in a normal tone of voice. I recognize this as being a result of Alzheimer's and not an expression of anger at me, although I am certainly the brunt of her outbursts. I try to maintain a calm attitude, but don't always succeed.

I guess the principal point of anyone's anger is to raise the ire in your antagonist, and Donna's anger gets more and more barbed until she can achieve a reaction from me. Part of her morning anger has been centred on her growing reluctance to take any pills. She even refuses to take a Tylenol, which helps with her arthritis issues. I might insist, but these days I can insist all I like and who knows if she actually takes the pills.

On other days, I use the afternoon for an opportunity for us both to go grocery shopping. Trips to go shopping often result in a kind of temper tantrum while in Save-On. Every time we shop, Donna finds dozens of things she would like to buy; she always wants some apples to add to the hoard of uneaten apples in our fridge. She is bedazzled by all the colourful displays. But with most of the things she pulls from the shelves my reaction is "NO! Not that!" Telling Donna no raises her anger, and a tantrum ensues where she refuses to follow me, and regularly gets lost in the store. Fortunately, all the workers in Save-On know Donna, and they very graciously steer her back to me, often in tears for having lost me.

Our world has changed again. I cannot go shopping or anywhere and leave Donna behind any more. She gets very nervous and anxious, even at home, if I am out of her sight for a minute. I use the bedroom and bathroom downstairs now, sometimes just as a sanctuary, an opportunity to calm myself down and clear my head. When I leave, within a minute, she no longer knows where I went and begins calling and searching for me. And she can't really find her way around the house. She forgets where all the rooms are and what they are called.

The late afternoons are taken up by me preparing our dinner. Cooking is still my love, and I find I can hustle around the kitchen with Donna in tow, and really enjoy preparing recipes that I would normally only do when company is coming. This is my relief and joy. And it's often done to Donna's growing frustration because I am not paying enough attention to her. These days, Donna doesn't like any food she doesn't recognize, and little of what I prepare…at least, that's what she says. But she certainly enjoys everything she eats. Well, usually! Perhaps, due to Alzheimer's, if Donna doesn't recognize the food on her plate, then it isn't food. Only after I coax her to try a little does she recognize the taste; her smile returns and she happily eats.

We take our dinner with our glass of wine (Donna drinks mostly apple juice these days) up to the TV room and watch something really exciting, like "Ellen DeGeneres" or "Mrs. Brown's Boys." If Donna gets angry at me because she can't help in dinner preparation anymore,

Donna's Story

that anger typically dissipates through dinner until bedtime, which is usually around 9:00 PM. About fifty percent of the time, Donna is very tired. Once I see she is in bed, I turn out the lights, come down and tidy up the kitchen dishes, then head to bed myself at about nine-thirty or ten. The other fifty percent of the time, Donna is extremely anxious about climbing into bed on her own, particularly with all those other women in the room.

Oh, yes! There is no more talk about two Johns in her life. Now there are two or more Donnas. She sees another woman in the mirror, and I often find them talking to each other. Naturally, I only hear Donna's side of the conversation. Quiet moments occur while her imaginary mirror image is replying. She knows her name is Donna, but she sees the image as a real person. A month ago, I thought these hallucinations were just a group of unidentified people in her mind, but I now see they are principally reflections of herself in the mirror.

So for the future, our world must evolve once again. We cannot continue with Donna "attached to my right hip" for every waking hour. I need some personal space, and there are things to do in which Donna need not, and often cannot, participate. But maybe some respite is coming, since we have both recently been re-introduced to Elva. Elva is a retired nurse who danced at Footloose as part of Donna's "Golden Girls" class. Elva has helped Donna in times gone by and has recently volunteered some of her time to come and work with Donna. She visited a week or so ago and again this past Monday when I met with Donna's case manager. Elva and I are now in the process of setting up similar visits in the weeks to come so I can plan to do some things independent of Donna. Elva is suggesting (and I am hoping) that she will be able to coax Donna into letting Elva shampoo her hair during her next visit. Donna won't let me do it and she doesn't do it herself!

Donna is scheduled for her annual physical next month and her GP has also suggested she have a colonoscopy, mainly because she was in Emergency a couple of months back suffering from diverticulosis—a complaint of the bowel. But considering Donna's dwindling respect for all her doctors and their ministrations, I am convinced she will not submit to a colonoscopy.

And I know she will not submit to a mammogram. Because of her previous bout with breast cancer she has to have a more strenuous mammogram than usual. I am thinking that, apart from the bloodwork done as part of the annual physical, Donna should forego the more invasive tests. When I discuss this with her doctor he accepts, but I don't think he agrees.

So I finally come to my meeting with Donna's case manager. When I arrive, I am convinced I am going to register Donna and get her on the list for permanent care. I want to ensure that even though Donna is still living with me, I will be able to obtain a sense of urgency from Fraser Health when the time comes. We discuss the waiting lists and the various places in the Fraser Health region.

Her case manager tells me that the waiting lists are typically eight to twelve months, and that when the location is offered it is expected to be accepted. If not accepted, she will be back at the end of the list and her priority will be lowered. His suggestion is to not list Donna today, but to reassess her every four months. When that assessment says she is ready, the priority can be raised to an urgent level. Fraser Health wants to place individuals in homes when sensible but, on the other hand, does not want to find it necessary to hospitalize an individual who is waiting for placement. So I again procrastinate and reschedule another assessment for September.

Finally, the case manager is encouraging me to make use of the home help available. A care worker will come in on a scheduled basis for a four-hour shift where I will be free to do whatever I need to do. It's time I paid some heed to this option, and I will be fitting that in over the months to come, along with the help from Elva.

Shortly after this meeting with Donna's case manager, I receive a beautiful and sensitive letter from my brother, Steve, and his wife Brenda, trying their best to let me know they think my decision to postpone is wrong. I really want to thank them both for their very thoughtful words. It must have been difficult to try and knock some sense into me.

I also have a long talk with Donna's brother, Bruce, and his wife Shirley, who essentially say the same thing. I talk to Elva again and I have a long meeting with my lawyer discussing wills and future care issues. The conclusions from you all are, "I have procrastinated long enough." You are all correct.

The action of committing Donna to an institution is extremely difficult and painful for me. I've known the moment would come from that first day back in 2009, but when it comes to actually taking the action, I simply don't want to do it. It means I am losing my life's companion.

But I have pulled my next meeting with Fraser Health forward to July, where I will put Donna on the necessary lists.

JULY

My Fraser Health meeting scheduled for July is shelved because Donna's case manager receives a promotion and transfers to another location. No new case manager has been assigned. After a few anxious words with Fraser Health and a short period of waiting, a new case manager arrives at our home to perform another assessment of Donna prior to listing her.

I am pleased to say that my concerns about being assigned a rookie, without skills and knowledge of Alzheimer's, were unfounded. The meeting goes well and as planned. Christine, a recently retired case manager, has returned to work two days per week. She is a mature ex RN who shows she has a sound understanding of Alzheimer's. She has lots of patience with Donna, and Donna takes to her as well. Christine will not be Donna's new case manager, but she will ensure issues are expedited in the interim. I ask Donna's friend Elva to participate in this meeting because I respect her opinions and, with Elva present, there is opportunity for me to have separate, private conversations with Christine.

The meeting begins with Christine explaining that the assessment is really just a formality and all the appropriate information is already on Donna's file. She has been in touch with Donna's doctors at the geriatric clinic and has read all Donna's history. Christine is well versed in the current state of her well-being, and needs only one little glance at Donna's tax return to clarify the appropriate rate structure. By scheduling her into care through Fraser Health, the outlandish rates for private care can be reduced to work within Donna's income. For this reason, it is necessary for them to see her tax return.

Christine is with us for a little over an hour, and most of that time is spent with me crossing T's and dotting I's about what facilities are available, how current and clean they are, and how caring the staff might be. I have stated I would like to consider facilities in Coquitlam and Burnaby only. Others are too far away to allow me to visit daily. I am very happy with our meeting, as is Elva.

On the fifteenth of August, Donna is registered and listed for permanent residential care. The expectation is she will be settled by the end of the year.

So my next job is to begin conversations with Donna on the above topic as well as planning visits to one or two facilities.

AUGUST

Life at home these days is exceedingly boring for Donna (as it is for me). She constantly asks, "What should I do?" There is nothing she can do! I must now guide her around the house because, although she is familiar with all the things in our house and can physically navigate her way around, she has no idea what the rooms are and how they fit together. She doesn't know where the kitchen is, or what its purpose is in our home. She doesn't know what or where the fridge is, nor her bedroom, nor the bathroom. She gets confused between upstairs and downstairs, and is beginning to dislike the bathroom and bedroom, for what reason I don't know. She gets frightened going to bed when I turn the light off—she's a little afraid of the dark, and of being alone in bed at night.

Donna now sees herself as Donna Frame (her maiden name), and not Donna Knapp. She regularly talks to her mirror "Donnas" and it sometimes surprises me, as I think she is talking to me. On many occasion, she has tried to bring her "Donna" into the room so she can introduce her to me.

Donna spends the morning going through her closet of clothes and shoes, getting surprised when she discovers a shirt that she takes a liking to. She doesn't know who owns it, and doesn't believe me when I tell her she has owned it for years. She has lots of clothes and lots of shoes (at least by my reckoning), but she really only wears one or two pairs of pants, about four shirts, and one or two pairs of shoes. But she usually has a field day with her panty-liners. Multiple liners often plastered over various parts of her clothing and body—only rarely located where they should be.

Everything Donna wants to do, I must do for her. I get her glasses of juice or milk many times in the day. Of course, I feed her. I need to cut up her meat into bite-sized pieces as she has a great deal of trouble with a knife and fork. I have to help her get dressed in the morning, not to put her clothes on, but to help her decide what to wear, and to sort out the complexity of deciding what piece of apparel needs to go on next. If I don't do this, it will be hours before she gets herself dressed.

The afternoon is usually taken up with small shopping trips to Save-On, etc., or with visits from friends, and now it also includes visits from Home Help. I have one person coming every Tuesday from Fraser Health, and Elva visiting every second Wednesday. I am finding the Home Help visits very valuable and can begin to think of things to do that don't include Donna. My enjoyment of writing short stories is rejuvenating, and I look forward to seeing how that develops over the coming months.

Donna now dislikes our shopping trips and, as I have reported in the past, trips to Save-On usually include a bit of a tantrum because she doesn't like me saying no to her so often. Her anger is a daily event. Maybe more than once in any day.

In defense of Donna, I have begun to analyze myself at these times. During the day, Donna's conversation is incessant, as she repeatedly removes the contents of her purse and asks me to describe each component before she puts it back. Time after time! Her mouth just doesn't stop. This gets very tiring for me, my anxiety rises, and I find myself getting angry with her, and I know I contribute to her anger. Anger wins out and we both must relieve it. About a half-hour later, I hear Donna, in tears, whispering to herself, "I just can't help it!" That's when I melt. Of course she can't help it.

In the early evening, I leave the living room to prepare dinner. Donna volunteers to help, but its only words. I find something simple for her

Donna's Story

to do. She asks me what she must do, but if I make the mistake of telling her she gets angry and returns to the living room. And by now I'm sure you all know, "NO-ONE... Repeat...NO-ONE! tells Donna what to do!" For dinner, we retire with our trays of dinner and begin an evening of TV. Entertainment shows prevail, providing they aren't contests requiring some thought, analysis and memory of what has just passed.

As we approach bedtime, I can see Donna's anxiety begin to rise. If I am smart at this time, I coax her to take a tiny little Seroquel and within a few minutes it works its charm. Donna calms down and we begin the ritual of preparing for bed. It always begins with a bathroom visit and other delays. Eventually, I can encourage her to remove her shoes—a little later followed by her pants. Usually that's as far as I get, and she climbs into bed with her shirt, underwear and socks. She no longer likes to wear her nighties. The process of going to bed takes about three-quarters of an hour and when she finally climbs in I sit in the chair beside her and turn out her light. This results in a kind of fearful shock. But I sit with her a while and soon she relaxes; I kiss her goodnight and head to bed myself.

Today, I think Donna is beginning to experience problems of the latter stages of Alzheimer's—deteriorating body motor functions. Overnight, I occasionally find the results of bathroom failures. By morning, of course, Donna remembers nothing.

And by morning, we are up and going through the process all over again. It is always the same!

SEPTEMBER

A time for a little reflection.

I just re-read Donna's Story from this time last year, mainly to get some sense of the changes in our lives, and especially the changes in Donna's general well-being over the year. At that time, I said that the year 2014 was the hardest so far. It was! But I also predicted that 2015 would be harder. It has been! And I know that if I do nothing, 2016 will be even more difficult.

Making the decision to put Donna in a care home has been difficult, but necessary; if I don't, this could kill me. I haven't the strength to continue as Donna's sole caregiver and if I try, the constant emotional impact on me will eventually bring on physical problems that will break me.

So here I am in September, just waiting until Fraser Health finds some accommodation, which will probably not be until January.

A year ago, I was able to leave Donna at home for an hour or two without the worry that she might wander or have an anxiety attack during my absence. I managed to get a little respite, albeit just shopping for groceries, or the occasional visit to my doctor, etc. Donna was still enjoying her dance classes and was managing reasonably well. She was playing the piano a little too, and still enjoying bridge with her friends. Visits to others that included dinners and evenings of conversation were beginning to become difficult, but there were also still some successes. I enjoyed preparing and cooking meals for the two of us, with Donna able to participate a little with the preparation. Her hallucinations and mood swings were only just beginning.

At that time, I took for granted the mental respite I received from those hour-long shopping trips, and didn't recognize their therapeutic value. I didn't see the need for the offered "Home Help" from Fraser Health. I was strong; I loved Donna; I could take care of her.

This year, all of that has changed. As long as Donna is awake, I cannot be out of her sight. She can do nothing for herself. I have to help her dress, a real challenge because I have no idea what she will agree to wear. Getting undressed for bed is even harder. Where I used to be able to help and guide her, she now gets angry and will often go to bed fully clothed. I have to show her where the bathroom is ten times a day, pick up her soiled underwear almost every morning, all the time listening to her angry abuse. Daily life is very exhausting for me.

Donna doesn't much care for any of the food I prepare and really doesn't like any exotic dishes. This has affected my joy of cooking and restricts the variety of things I try. Many things I did in the kitchen a year ago I no longer make. I find myself serving pizza a little too frequently, but I do still try to keep our meals balanced—lots of vegetables. Of course, Donna cannot participate in the preparatory work anymore.

I get extremely frustrated with the prison we are both in, and I often get angry. I know that some of those shouting sessions between us are started by me, and I regularly find I must disappear down to my bedroom for a half-hour or so to relieve my anxieties and calm down. It isn't difficult to recognize when my anxieties reach unacceptable heights. My left arm begins to ache—not a good sign!

This year I have discovered, a little surprisingly, that my body takes far longer to recover than expected and I am definitely weaker than I was a year ago. I have a weakened heart and suffer from blood pressure ills. I have medication for this and carry a puffer of nitroglycerin in case of an angina attack. Remarkably, through all those experiences in

Emergency back in March, I did not have to use the nitro puffer at all. One small good sign.

But through that long period of recuperation, I took my eye off the ball regarding Donna's care. I procrastinated, and failed to register her when I should have. But now, plans for Donna's care are back on track; she is listed for care, and her legal/financial position is settled. We are both back to a kind of waiting game—waiting for some action from Fraser Health.

But where my anxieties reduced back in August when I committed to the plan, they are now beginning to rise again. I need to set up a trust to manage Donna's care should I die, but I can't quite do that yet because our assets are principally locked into the value of our home, and do not exist in any bank account or investment. And what about MY legal and financial situation? To protect Donna, I must set up Power of Attorney and Rep 9 Agreements on myself as well, to ensure that others can act on my behalf should I become incapacitated and unable to answer for myself. My lawyer and my bank are again called into action to set up those facilities with my brother Dave named as my attorney. All this takes time, so September is very busy, and, as I said, my anxieties are again on the rise to the point where my left arm begins to ache on a fairly regular basis.

Brother Dave steps in once again, thankfully, and gives me a much-needed kick in the ass. "What are you doing about your failing health?" he asks.

OCTOBER – NOVEMBER

In the first days of October, my anxieties are climbing to new heights. I am experiencing sharp pains in my lower left abdomen, right where my one remaining kidney resides. Immediate action is needed! I must check in to Emergency and get some help. Donna has to go into temporary respite care, right now.

Fraser Health quickly responds, raises Donna to the state of "Urgent" and offers her two weeks in temporary respite care while I see about my abdominal pain. Donna goes back to Delta View Centre, where she stayed back in March. I take her in on the seventh of October and then check into hospital to examine my abdominal issues. No kidney malfunction, and a course of antibiotics slowly removes my pain—probably psychosomatic. Next, I'm off to the cardiologist for treadmill tests, and coming soon, carotid artery checks for blockages, and possible stents to bypass cholesterol buildup.

On the day before I am to pick up Donna from respite care, I receive a call from George Derby Centre. They have a room available for Donna in permanent residential care. Fraser Health has reacted quickly again, but what am I to do? My anxiety is through the roof. I know it's time to act—NOW, and I'm just plain scared! But I do act, and the next day becomes my worst day in seventy-four years of memories.

On the twenty-second of October, I pick up Donna from her respite care centre and drive directly to George Derby without coming home. George Derby is a frenetic environment with eighty residents everywhere, and not enough nurses and care workers. In tears, Donna asks me, "Can I come home with you?" and I have to tell her, "No." My parting with her on that day is horrific.

Donna is at a point in her disease where she needs attention and care twenty-four hours a day, and for two weeks she endures that environment, showing lots of aggression and anger. They want no visitors so they can have time to help Donna settle in with her new care workers.

After two weeks, George Derby finds her too much to handle and hints that maybe I should bring her back home. I'm in terrible anguish over this. I'm so ready to bring her home. But absolutely everyone I talk to, including Fraser Health, says "That is the wrong thing to do. She is now in the hands of the Provincial Health Care system where she must stay." If I bring her home, she will be dropped to the bottom of the priority list, and it will probably take another year before placement can be found, when we will have to go through this process again.

Eventually, my left brain kicks in and I know they are right. Everyone needs more time to let things settle down. George Derby moves Donna upstairs to their special care unit and begins to sedate her slightly. Again, a new bed and care workers to get used to. Another two weeks of aggressive behavior, but slowly Donna begins to settle. They still don't want me to visit. To be frank, I am frightened about the prospect of visiting her. I'm beginning to feel as if I never want to visit. I couldn't bear to repeat that first day when I left her being physically restrained by the care workers while I slipped away; both of us in tears.

Finally, on the sixteenth of November, they allow visitors. However, I am still not ready. But reports from those friends who do manage a visit are all good, and on the twentieth, thanks to our friend Marylynn, I finally get up courage and make my first visit. It's the first time I really sit and talk with Donna since the seventh of October. That meeting is wonderful! I take along some of her favourite pictures and our wedding album for her to enjoy, as well as some additional clothes. Apparently, loss of belongings is typical in these places.

For the balance of November, I am unable to visit because I have contracted the flu. I haven't had a cold or flu for over twenty-five years and am again forced to recognize my reduced state of health.

DECEMBER

Through the month of December, I visit Donna many times. I feel that despite the fact they are sedating her daily, Donna is basically in a happy place. The highlight of her day is the sing-a-long sessions where she entertains everyone, sings songs and teaches other residents to dance. Our visits are great, and I usually leave her singing songs with Carlos, one of the care workers. I see her again tomorrow, and will take along her boom-box and some CDs for her to listen and sing along to. I no longer have any anxieties about visiting her, and am pleased with the level of care exhibited by the George Derby staff.

I still have a very emotional reaction to all these events—lots of black moments when I stop and think of our life together. It's all gone now, with only me to remember the happier times, but as each day passes, the black moments are getting shorter and fewer. I am fairly sure that Donna has no such black memories. She certainly seems happy.

Reflections on the future!

It is very early yet to reflect on what is to come. Life at home is suddenly much quieter. It is also lonely. I have never lived alone in my entire life, and it is a little scary. I feel I must open up to new horizons and activities. I still enjoy writing, but that is a very solitary activity and I need more human contact.

I soon see that our home is now too much for me; there are too many memories. I plan to sell it in the coming spring, but I'm not in any hurry. I don't really know what I want to do or where I want to go. I have thought about moving up to Kelowna near my brother Dave and his family, a good idea that I was happier with when I thought I might not visit Donna. I don't feel that way today. I also thought I might move to Granville Island. I like the excitement of all the people, the market, the theatres, etc. But that would mean leaving everything and everyone I know here in Coquitlam or nearby. And do I want another house, townhome, apartment or condo? I need more time to reflect.

The cost of Donna's care is substantial right now and beyond our joint budget, but after I wrangle out all the wrinkles with the tax office I think I can reduce the rate to a manageable sum. But other financial issues are looming. What are the implications now that Donna is not living with me and is perhaps no longer considered my dependent? What happens to the disability tax credit? I still need to set up a trust to guarantee Donna's support in the event of my death, and that can't be done until I sell our home.

For the immediate future, I plan to stay in our home, but our garden that Donna so liked to wander through is no longer interesting to me—there is no one to share it with.

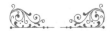

2016 – CALM AFTER THE STORM JANUARY TO APRIL

I, and a few friends and relatives, visit Donna over the Christmas week. We bring her downstairs to the "Town Hall" to enjoy some Christmas carolers and Santa Claus. Donna enjoys an hour and a half, with the first real smile on her face since entering care, and I begin to relax. George Derby has sing-a-long events each Wednesday and Saturday, and if I can make it on those days, I again bring Donna downstairs to enjoy the scene. She is sometimes quiet and morose when I first make my appearance; I often have difficulty persuading her to come downstairs with me. But when we get to the "Town Hall" and the singing begins, there is a dramatic change in her. I just sit in the centre of the big room sipping my beer and watch as Donna cruises the room, dancing everywhere and with everyone, smiling, singing, shaking hands and talking to everyone—residents, care workers and visitors. Everyone knows her name, calls out to her, and everyone smiles. Donna is happy. The care workers tell me they are so thankful for Donna's activity, because she helps even the most comatose resident to perk up, smile and hold a hand out to her, even if just for a minute.

However pleasant these times are, they still only reflect a very short time in any week. Donna can usually be found quietly sitting with her eyes half closed and not very responsive to my visits. On many occasions I just sit beside her and hold her hand, sometimes with hardly a word spoken in an hour. Other times, she might fall asleep and I just leave, even if it's only been a fifteen-minute visit.

In January, a new resident joins Donna's special care unit. Sue is practically the only other young resident on the ward, being just sixty-five years old. Donna, now seventy-one, and Sue, become immediate friends, and Donna calls Sue her boyfriend. They talk together all the time and, although I listen carefully, I can't make out a word they are saying. But they seem to understand each other. I call Donna, Sue and another resident, Marilyn, the three musketeers. They regularly patrol the halls ensuring residents, care workers, and nurses alike, toe the line and answer to their every need, immediately.

Huge credit has to be offered to the George Derby staff. They all maintain a continuous "up" attitude, know all the residents and greet them by name whenever they pass in the halls. Their task is a thankless one, being caregivers to twenty-three dementia residents who typically don't appreciate their ministrations. Caregivers often receive a lot of abuse, and yes! Donna is occasionally one of those abusers. I could not do the care worker's job. Caring day after day as their residents slowly fade away, none of them ever recovering. Through it all, they maintain their smiling and happy attitude towards everyone—each other, visitors, and residents—even the abusive ones.

Alzheimer's patients need a lot of one-on-one attention, even during the night. There is never enough staff to offer that level of care, so they regularly sedate each resident. Donna is given Seroquel three times a day, and I sometimes feel that because of that, Donna is often in an overly subdued mood. Seroquel is not a nice drug, and I ask her doctor about it periodically to see if it is absolutely necessary. I saw him again a few days ago and he has agreed to try to reduce Donna's dosage. A lot will depend on how it affects Donna's behaviour.

I still occasionally have the urge to pack Donna up and bring her home. But then I think of the two environments—George Derby vs our home. At home, she would be confined to our bedroom, bathroom, living room and kitchen. I would not be able to let her out of my sight for a minute, day or night, meaning that I, too, couldn't leave the house. I could no longer take her shopping or visit friends. She would have no one to talk to except me.

At George Derby, she has twenty-three residents and about ten care workers that offer her plenty of social contact, an important factor in someone as gregarious as Donna is now. For me, George Derby offers respite, freedom from worry and freedom to continue a normal (if different) life. For Donna, George Derby offers a more sociable, larger and happier environment—a better life than the life I could provide for her. More and more I know I have made the right decision.

Through it all, I do notice her continuing on this slow path of deterioration. Now, in April, she is not as active in the "Town Hall" as she was in January. Except for the two or three younger women I spoke about earlier, most of the other residents are much older—in their late eighties or nineties. They are much less active than Donna, often just sitting in one place for an hour or more, saying nothing, not truly cognizant unless someone speaks to them. And I can see the path ahead will bring Donna slowly to this same state. It frightens me, but there is nothing I can do except enjoy the moments that remain. She is basically healthy, eating well, and even putting on a little weight.

Donna still recognizes me and other close friends immediately, although she sometimes stumbles over the task of finding the right name. It really doesn't matter. She is always more than happy to receive all visitors, even if she doesn't remember who you are. Her eyes light up and conversation begins. The ebullience probably only lasts for thirty or forty minutes, but in that time she experiences joy. Just don't tell her what to do!

My heart goes out to Donna and everyone at her care centre.

As for me, I completed all my cardio tests in January (including the various dreaded MIBI treadmill tests). The result? No significant cholesterol buildup on any arteries. No stents. My cardiologist made a minor change to my blood pressure medication and sent me home. Every day, I can recognize the decrease in my stress levels, and I feel my strength improving. I sold our home in February for a princely sum that will ensure that both Donna and I have a comfortable senior life.

I have chosen a new home that is much smaller. It is a two-bedroom condo, in an area that offers lots of walking opportunities in a local park, shops nearby, and access to our intercity rapid transit system, meaning I will be able to reach most parts of our city via public transport. I move to my new condo in May to a new life full of youth, children and hundreds of dogs.

Donna is in the best place she could be and she's happy to be there.

MAY – AUGUST

Well, my move to my condo went smoothly in May. I am settled, feeling stronger, and noticeably free of most of my anxieties over Donna. I have set up her trust fund so she can remain comfortable at her care centre for the rest of her days. My "house" is in financial order. I do not have to worry about Donna's care in the event I die before she does. Brother Dave and his wife, Barb, have agreed to be my attorneys in case that course of action is required. My lawyer and my bank know all about them—they brought them in, took photographs, and possibly fingerprints, and pronounced them acceptable. Donna's brother, Bruce, has agreed to manage Donna's trust with Fraser Health in the event of my death.

It may sound like morbid thinking, but now that these aspects are resolved I can relax and start putting my life back in order, where it ought to be. It will take time.

At the moment, I am the victim of my own brain. I have erratic sleep patterns, lying awake for a couple of hours each night with my mind still a-turmoil; I find my dreams a bit too livid. I often see Donna in my dreams now. Each one is different, but Donna is always young, beautiful and vibrant; always dressed in the latest fashions, and making her own way in her life—without me! For some unexplained reason, she has left me. She is sophisticated and travels the world. Occasionally our paths cross, and when we meet, I always have to look twice to make sure she is truly Donna. We are friendly and cordial with each other, but I cannot touch her, cannot reach her heart. Then I wake with a terrible feeling of sadness.

Unlike most dreams, these dreams stay with me upon waking and do not disappear. I realize they are fraught with symbolism, my brain's way of helping me forget, helping me cope with my loss—or perhaps my brain's way of ensuring I remember.

I'm way more socially active than I was even four months ago. I do find I'm dining out a little too much, but I really think I owe it to my new community to investigate the local eateries: the bistros, craft breweries and ethnic palaces, as well as the occasional elegant dining emporia. Like younger people today, I don't have a dining room, so I cook for others much less than I used to. That's okay, because my kitchen is tiny, and I only have a fraction of the cooking gear I once had.

Downsizing has been tougher than I thought. I'm not quite finished, either, as I still have a coffee table and two end tables to coax into the loving arms of a niece, nephew or friend. I enjoy walking to my nearby shops etc., although I don't yet walk enough. I have joined the strata council to try and have some say in how my new abode is managed. We'll see how that plays out over the coming months.

So, how has Donna been faring over the past few months?

I notice quite a change, certainly since she entered George Derby last October. After the settling in period, she is clearly happier than she had been when home with me over the previous year. She has lots of people to talk to and dance with; people who listen to her, who don't tell her to do things (except when she misbehaves), and who clearly like her. Not just the staff, but the residents also respect and understand her.

But I noticed more changes through May and June. And today, in July, it's a little different again. I visit her about three times a week and I notice that when I take her downstairs to the "Town Hall" she doesn't dance around the room as much. But she still sings her heart out. In April, I asked her doctor if they could reduce the amount of Seroquel they give Donna because, at that time, I felt she was often in a cloud, nearly asleep, and not very cognizant of her world. Soon after they reduced the drug I saw a new sparkle in her eyes, more smiles and more dancing and singing. That new sparkle isn't always there, but I think her slow-down today is more related to the Alzheimer's than the sedatives.

Donna's motor skills are noticeably dwindling. Her walking pace is very slow, with her feet pointing out like duck's feet (or a ballet dancer's feet—sorry, all you dancers). She stops and stands often, and needs coaching to start again. We occasionally walk around her small garden, and it becomes quite an effort of prodding and coaxing to make it all the way around.

She seems to have difficulty getting from a sitting position to standing. That is probably because someone (like me) is trying to help her, and she gets frightened she will lose balance. But she seems to manage okay when she does it herself. Her standing posture has changed. She now stands leaning back a little with weight on her heels. Being a dancer, that's just not Donna. As a result, she is much less steady on her feet. Just yesterday, while dancing in the "Town Hall," her feet got tangled and she fell. She was wearing hip pads and her head didn't hit the floor, so after a careful check of her basic motor functions by her nurse, Doris, together we managed to help her back to her feet. She rested in a chair for a whole five minutes until the music started. Then her feet started tapping and she was up, cruising the entire room again, obviously in no physical pain. She's lucky. She's basically healthy, and doesn't suffer from osteoporosis.

It has also been reported to me lately that Donna has been discovered during the night sitting on her bedroom floor leaning against her bed happily singing. Each incident is treated by the care workers as a fall and Donna is taken through the various tests for head and body trauma. Everything okay so far.

Donna's bathroom habits have changed too. She cannot manage toilets on her own, and always needs assistance. She wears padded underwear because her body gives her practically no notice that she needs to use the facilities. If she doesn't get to a bathroom within about thirty seconds, an accident happens.

Her conversations are far fewer than only a couple of months ago. She talks to others much less frequently—me as well as nurses or other residents. This, I am sure, is because of the lack of retention of what she has just said or what others have said to her. Or perhaps it's just the Alzheimer's robbing her of her ability to formulate words and sentences. She still enjoys my company, doesn't want me to leave and is content that I just sit beside her without talking. The days of her patrolling the halls with the other two musketeers, Sue and Marilyn, seem to be over.

A week or two ago, George Derby celebrated Canada Day with a summer barbeque. Donna had a great deal of trouble managing her cheeseburger. Marylynn and I were trying to coach her to just pick the whole thing up and take a big bite. She couldn't manage that. She had to take the entire burger apart and eat each part separately in small bites. Other residents had the same problem. Finger skills, along with knife and fork skills, are all dwindling.

Donna is now having a little trouble eating in general. Her care workers are saying she is often reluctant to take a bite of food. One thing that happens as Alzheimer's progresses is that the brain forgets to turn on the "I'm hungry" switch. It sounds silly to us, because we never even consider those automatic functions our brain provides. When we need sustenance, our brain turns on the hunger pangs, and we react. It never crosses our minds that there is a function in our bodies, controlled by our brain, that tells us we are ready to eat— and another function that tells us we are full, and eating can stop. This feature allows us to maintain a stable weight. When Donna doesn't get hunger pangs, she sees those trying to encourage her to eat as aggressors. And remember…never tell Donna what to do!

Care workers have asked me to bring in something for Donna to eat; they think perhaps I can persuade her to take a nibble of something she likes, where the care workers might fail. Three months ago I commented that Donna was gaining weight. She is now losing a little weight.

Donna's Story

Donna has lots of up days when she is happy about going down to the "Town Hall." Her eyes again sparkle and we have a good time for an hour and a half or two hours. That is absolutely the maximum excitement she can manage. It is then a slow process to get her back upstairs and into a chair. On other days, she sits in the lunch room sound asleep with head back, snoring away. No one can wake her, and I leave within a few minutes.

A warm thing I have recently noticed is that the residents consider themselves part of a family. They like each other, comfort and protect each other. Yesterday, when I was trying to help Donna out of her chair to head downstairs, she was resisting a little. Resident Alex slowly came over to us, put his hand on my arm as if to stop me, turned to Donna and asked, "Are you okay?"

I was surprised, in no way offended, and responded for Donna, "Oh yes! I'm planning to take her downstairs where she can dance."

He turned back to Donna and asked, "Is that what you want to do?"

He only let go of my arm when Donna said, "Yes!" It was a touching moment.

Of course, there are other moments when one resident has a violent outburst towards another that sometimes comes to threatened blows. A care worker has to be quick to step between them. These events occur more often during a full moon than at other times. That is well known at George Derby.

On our way downstairs in the elevator today, Donna and I were accompanied by wheelchair bound resident, Americo, and his care worker. Americo, sounding typically Italian, boldly proclaimed to me, "Do you know what Donna said to me the other day? She said, 'I have a husband, you know!'" We all laughed, but it got me thinking what the circumstances might have been to solicit a comment like that from Donna. Just because they are in various stages of Alzheimer's disease doesn't mean the libido is no longer active. I told Americo I was going to change his name to "Amoroso" because I thought he was just a little too amorous. He laughed too; he knew what it meant in Italian, and was not displeased. And Donna is not his only quest.

I see the pace of Donna's regression increasing. Her troubles are beginning to affect the motor skills area in the rear of her brain, and changes are occurring more rapidly. I can do nothing but wait, observe and do my best to ensure her days are comfortable.

SEPTEMBER – DECEMBER

I come now to the last months of 2016. This will also be the last chapter of Donna's Story. If I were to continue the story, I would just be repeating similar events, so it's time to summarize. But be assured! It is definitely not Donna's last chapter—not our last chapter. We are both still together on that mountain road. Today, she is not quite "with it," so to speak. She's still active, alert and basically healthy, although she obviously continues to slowly regress.

I check her general well-being regularly. What is her care plan? How is she sleeping? Are her fingernails and toenails kept trimmed and clean? Is her medication necessary and in the right dosage? Does she need any more clothes, shoes, nighties, etc.? How is her health—generally? What are her teeth like? Is she getting regular showers and hair washing? Haircuts? Are her five senses still working effectively? Stuff like that.

In September, I bought her a wheelchair. I use the chair to help take her on small excursions: out to the garden or down to the "Town Hall" to do some singing and dancing. She still gets excited when the singing begins.

She doesn't need the wheelchair for daily use because she's still ambulatory, even if she walks the "Alzheimer's walk!" As long as no-one is trying to help, she gets herself from sitting to standing with very little difficulty. She proceeds to walk—in no particular direction, or a direction known only to herself. After about twenty paces, she stops, stares straight ahead and waits for a minute or so. Then she turns and walks some more—again, in no particular direction, having probably forgotten why she started walking in the first place. All the Alzheimer's residents in Donna's ward walk this way—even the very alert ones. It's a little exasperating to me, who is usually following, trying to guess where she is going and why.

October twenty-second marks Donna's anniversary of going into George Derby Centre—my "black" Wednesday. October twenty-eight marks her seventy-second birthday, and she is comfortable today.

Now, in December, this is Donna's second Christmas at George Derby, and I notice yet another change; perhaps a change due to a new phase of Alzheimer's disease, or perhaps a change resulting from a variation in her sedative medication. Donna has become much more affectionate towards me. As soon as I arrive, her eyes light up, her arms open wide for a big hug, she cuddles and squeezes me, and reaches up for a kiss, or two, or three. I am really liking this new phase.

But I have to add that this demonstrative behaviour is completely atypical of Donna. In our years together, she always reserved her affection for those moments when we were alone; never in public.

Today, I find Donna singing, dancing, laughing and chattering on every visit; not just at the "Town Hall." In addition to her new-found affection for me, she is also showing affection for her co-residents and care workers. She will talk to them all, put a hand on their shoulder, or stroke their arm, always with a big smile. On occasion, this is misinterpreted by a resident, so a care worker has to step in to ensure things remain on an even keel. These are all innocent events and I hope this phase lasts for a long time.

Christmas has passed and it is now the end of the year. I have had time to ease my anxieties and reflect on our lives over the past seven years. In the paragraphs that follow, I will attempt to write an objective summary while trying not to get maudlin or too philosophical. But I suspect I won't quite succeed.

Alzheimer's is a terrible disease. What it does to victims, caregivers, friends and relatives is force us all to recognize that we have a limited lifespan. We know we shall die eventually, but we successfully put that out of our mind until an unexpected event like disease, accident or some organ failure, brings us face to face with death. We, in the Western societies, have a very high love of life, and fear of death. We are not philosophical about it like some Eastern societies. Death is always a tragedy to us.

Whether of short or long duration, Alzheimer's disease forces us to stare death in the face much sooner than expected, and for a sometimes prolonged period of time. It is very painful. And one of the most painful aspects is the realization that we cannot stand side-by-side with our loved-one until the end. We simply don't have the tools or stamina to provide the care that is needed in the later stages of the disease. A care home is a very necessary step in the process, and the pressure of committing a loved one to an institution, even a good one, is very hard to master. There are not many consoling factors for those of us who are forced to remain on the sidelines and watch as the ones we love slowly, and inexorably, descend into a kind of abyss.

In the preceding chapters, I have often said that I didn't think Donna was in any physical pain or mental anguish. I am fairly certain about the physical pain, but I don't think I was right about mental anguish.

When I look back and think about her loss of memories; that is one thing. There were many experiences in Donna's memory about her life that are missing today. I don't suppose those memory losses have given her any anguish, because what is no longer there obviously isn't remembered, and so, never existed.

But I'm equally sure that, over the years, she did notice the slow disappearance of her cognitive and mechanical abilities. She always got extremely exasperated about her difficulties with social conversations, or with helping to prepare dinner— something simple, like cutting up carrots. She always got furious when she thought someone was telling her what to do. Those situations demonstrated problems with functions that she had always been able to manage without help, and she seemed to be at least partially aware that things were going wrong. Those feelings were probably responsible for her mood swings and general anger.

I have also spoken of the anger between us. On reflection, this has clearly been one of the products of Alzheimer's disease. In our earlier years together, there was never anger like we experienced over the Alzheimer's years. Oh, yes, of course there were occasional arguments, but we had a tacit understanding that disputes were always resolved before going to bed at night. I see now that her bouts of anger were simply a reflection of the mental anguish she was suffering.

Today, I do believe this mental anguish has abated. By a strange quirk, Alzheimer's itself has provided the beneficial tonic. As her brain cells are slowly destroyed, Donna's knowledge of the cognitive and mechanical skills she once enjoyed, diminishes. It no longer bothers her that she is incontinent, or that she has trouble standing up, or that she occasionally falls while dancing. Everything is today. Capabilities she enjoyed yesterday no longer mean anything to her, because they are not remembered. She is at peace with her world.

So what is to come? What are my expectations over the weeks and months ahead? In a past chapter, I described what can occur once the disease reaches the cerebellum, when basic motor functions fail and death is imminent. Alzheimer's doesn't usually take that long. It is more likely that Donna will succumb to more prosaic ailments, like pneumonia—brought on by Alzheimer's, of course. Perhaps a morsel of food goes down the wrong pipe into the lungs and cannot be dislodged. Perhaps the immune system malfunctions, or another disease strikes, and the army of red blood corpuscles aren't brought to the battle. Even a common cold can devolve into pneumonia.

Today, Donna is enduring the last remnants of a chest cold that has lingered for more than three weeks. She still has a loose raspy cough that frightens her. She doesn't understand. After every cough she asks her care worker, "What is happening in my chest?" She doesn't remember what a cough is.

I am taking her some probiotic drinks to hopefully spur the immune system into action to get rid of that cough.

Faults in her immune system are most certainly responsible for Alzheimer's disease in the first place, so there are many possible ways that Donna could eventually leave this world. No one knows how, or when, that might occur. I can only wait and see.

But I wait with the confidence that Donna, her mind, body, and soul, are finally, after seven years, in a happy place. Because of that, I, too, am in a happier place, and must not despair. And finally, you, reading this story, must not despair either. In your story, you too will find your happy place.

ABOUT THE AUTHOR

John and Donna were, and are, soul mates - sharing a mutual love of the arts, particularly music, and a deep curiosity about the world around them and its various cultures.

When John realized and finally accepted the fact that he was gradually losing his life-partner, his frustrations, anger, fear, and anxiety, led him to write of their experiences. Regular quarterly, sometimes monthly, e-mail 'updates' provided a way to keep friends and relatives informed as well as offering him some release from the stresses they both faced as their world slowly closed in around them.

Doctors seemed unable to tell him much about the progress of Donna's condition so John decided that by summarizing those e-mails and chronologically presenting their experiences in this book he believed he might be able to assist others going through the same confusion and fear.

> "Ultimately, some understanding and acceptance of Donna's situation was the critical first step towards my peace of mind."
>
> Sandra Pinner

CPSIA information can be obtained
at www.ICGtesting.com
Printed in the USA
VHW04s0730010618
579192LV00001B/15/P